Everyday English

Book 3
Second Edition

Barbara Zaffran
Staff Development Specialist in
ESL and Native Languages
New York City

David Krulik
Former Director
Secondary-School ESL Programs
New York City

Consulting Editor
Linda Schinke-Llano, Ph.D.

National Textbook Company
a division of NTC/CONTEMPORARY PUBLISHING GROUP
Lincolnwood, Illinois USA

*To Alain, with love
and remembrance*

Cover Photo Credits: Camerique (top right); Chip
and Rosa Maria de la Cueva Peterson (top left);
R. Krubner/H. Armstrong Roberts (bottom left);
ZEFA-U.K./H. Armstrong Roberts (bottom right)

ISBN: 0-8442-0662-8

Published by National Textbook Company,
a division of NTC/Contemporary Publishing Group, Inc.,
4255 West Touhy Avenue,
Lincolnwood (Chicago), Illinois 60712-1975 U.S.A.

0 1 2 3 4 5 6 7 8 9 VP 16 15 14 13 12 11 10 9

Contents

Unit 1 Our Community

Lesson 1   People and Places

Exercise 1   Study the following vocabulary with your teacher.

1. A *community* is made up of all the people in one area and the places they live and work in.

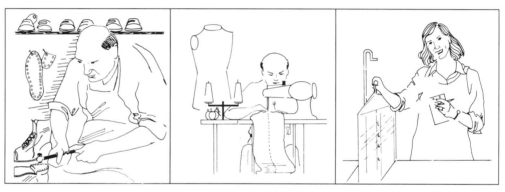

2. A *shoe repairer* is a person who fixes your shoes.

3. A *tailor* is a person who fixes your clothing.

4. A *dry cleaner* is a person who cleans clothes that can't be washed.

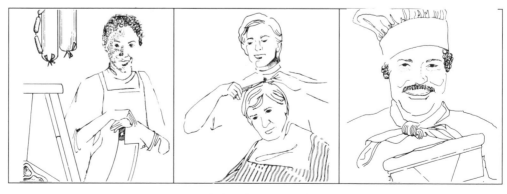

5. A *butcher* is a person who sells meat.

6. A *barber* or *stylist* is a person who cuts or styles hair.

7. A *baker* is a person who makes bread and cake.

8. A *store* is where you buy things.
9. A *department store* is a large store with many sections.
10. A *grocery store* is a store that sells food.
11. A *supermarket* is a very large grocery store.
12. A *bank* is where you keep your money.
13. A *hardware store* is a store that sells electrical and plumbing supplies and house paints.
14. A *laundromat* is a store where you can wash you clothes in a washing machine.
15. A *hairdresser's* is where women go to have their hair washed, cut, and styled. Men often go to either a hairdresser's or a barbershop.

Exercise 2   Circle the correct answer.

1. In a grocery store you can buy _____ .

   a. paint   b. canned food   c. clothes

2. A butcher is a person who sells _____ .

   a. fish   b. fruit   c. meat

3. A store is where you _____ .

   a. sit   b. eat   c. buy things

4. A bank is where you keep your _____ .

   a. clothes   b. money   c. books

5. In a hardware store you can buy _____ .

   a. nails   b. soup   c. books

6. A laundromat is where you _____ .

   a. fix clothes   b. wash clothes   c. wash hair

7. A baker makes _____ .

   a. meat   b. eggs   c. cake

8. A tailor is a person who _____ .

   a. fixes clothes   b. fixes shoes   c. cleans clothes

9. A barber is a person who _____ .

   a. makes bread   b. cuts hair   c. cuts meat

10. A shoe repairer _____ .

   a. sells shoes   b. fixes shoes   c. makes clothes

Exercise 3   Put the numbers of the stores, shops, and buildings in the appropriate blanks.

____ private house   ____ apartment house   ____ drugstore

____ bank   ____ school   ____ church

____ bakery   ____ dentist's office ____ doctor's office

____ police station ____ firehouse   ____ laundromat

____ hardware store ____ department store   ____ barbershop

Exercise 4   Take a walk around a few blocks near your school. Make a list of the stores and businesses you see.

1. _____

2. _____

3. _____

4. _____

5. _____

6. _____

7. _____

8. _____

9. _____

10. _____

Exercise 5   Answer the questions with complete sentences.

1. What is a community?_____

   _____

   _____

2. What do you find in a community?_____

   _____

   _____

3. What kinds of stores do you need in your community to make it better?

   _____

   _____

Lesson 2   Neighborhoods and Districts

Exercise 1   Read these paragraphs.

   Throughout the United States there are areas of large cities that have their own names, for example, Watts in Los Angeles, Beacon Hill in Boston, Lincoln Park in Chicago, and Soho in New York. These parts of the city are called *neighborhoods*. Can you name some neighborhoods in your city?

   Every city has different parts for different reasons. These parts are called *districts*. There are three kinds of districts: *industrial, business,* and *residential*. The industrial district contains factories and warehouses. The business district contains stores, offices, and banks. The residential district is where people live. There we see houses, schools, and churches.

Everyday English, Book Three

Exercise 2   Match column A and column B.

                    A   **B**

          ____ 1. neighborhood   a. factories

          ____ 2. industrial district   b. houses

          ____ 3. business district   c. community

          ____ 4. residential district   d. stores

Exercise 3   Complete the sentences.

1. Lincoln Park, Harlem, and Watts are examples of

   _____ .

2. The names of some neighborhoods in my city are _____

   _____ .

3. The name of my neighborhood is _____

4. Every town is made up of three kinds of _____ .

   They are the _____ ,

   _____ , and _____ .

5. In the residential district we find _____ ,

   schools, and _____ .

6. In the industrial district we find _____ .

7. In the business district we find _____ .

8. I live in a _____ district.

Exercise 4   Complete the sentences.

   a. 1. __ __ o r __   _____

      2. __ __ m __ u __ __ __ __   _____

      3. __ i __ t __ __ __ t   _____

      4. __ __ s __ __ __ s s   _____

b. 1. In the residential _____ we see many houses.

   2. A synonym for neighborhood is _____ .

   3. In the_____ district there are many stores.

   4. You can buy nails in the hardware_____ .

Exercise 5   Make a list of the buildings and services found in each of these districts in your town.

  a. industrial district

    1. _____

    2. _____

    3. _____

    4. _____

    5. _____

    6. _____

  b. business district

    1. _____

    2. _____

    3. _____

    4. _____

    5. _____

    6. _____

  c. residential district

    1. _____

    2. _____

    3. _____

    4. _____

    5. _____

    6. _____

Lesson 3 Directions

Exercise 1 Match column A and column B.

	A			B
____	1. east		a.	(compass pointing S)
____	2. near		b.	away
____	3. north		c.	(compass pointing E)
____	4. far		d.	close
____	5. south		e.	(compass pointing N)
____	6. west		f.	(compass pointing W)
____	7. map		g.	plan

Exercise 2 Look at the map and discuss it with your teacher.

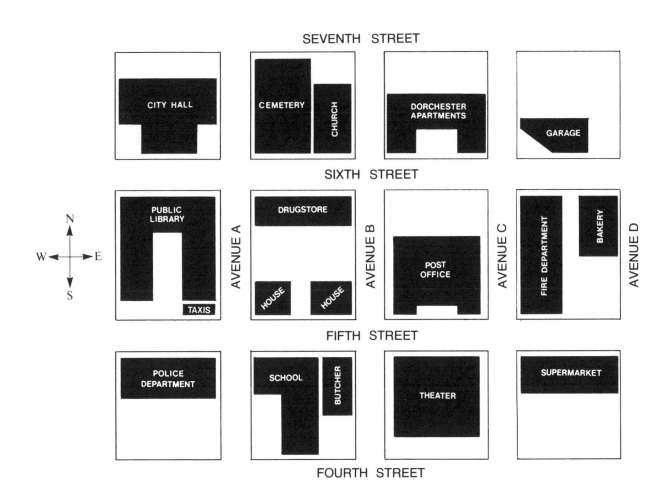

Read the following dialogues. Refer to the map as you read. Then answer the questions.

Visitor at City Hall: Where is a nice place to live in this community?

Clerk: The Dorchester Apartments. They're also on Sixth Street, just two blocks east of here. Also, there are some nice homes on Fifth Street, just one block south of here.

Student at library: How do I get to the movie theater from here?

Librarian: Go back to your school on Fifth Street. Then walk one block east. It will be on your right.

Driver at garage: I need to get a prescription filled while you work on my car. Where is the closest drugstore.

Repairman: Walk toward the church. The drugstore is right across the street.

Shopper in supermarket: Where can I find the post office?

Clerk: It's kitty-corner from here.

Woman at taxi stand: Is it far to the bakery?

Taxi driver: Well, it's three blocks east and one block north. It's not too far, but it looks like rain. Why not take a taxi?

Customer at post office: What is the address of the butcher's shop?

Clerk: It's 107 Avenue B.

Exercise 4

Look at the map and the dialogues to answer these questions.

1. Where can you live in this community? _____

   _____

2. What street is the movie theater on? _____

   _____

3. What is the drugstore across from? _____

4. What is kitty-corner from the supermarket? _____

5. How can you get from the taxi stand to the bakery? _____

   _____

6. What is kitty-corner from the drugstore? _____

7. What is across from the school? _____

8. What is east of the church? _____

9. What is west of the butcher's shop? _____

10. What is the address of the butcher's shop? _____

_____

Lesson 4 Review of Our Community

Exercise 1 Read the following paragraphs with your teacher.

Our community consists of many apartment houses and many stores. It is a residential and business district. On my block there are a bakery, a dry cleaner's, a shoe repair shop, a grocery store, and a drugstore. Around the corner from my house are the school I attend, the butcher's shop, and a laundromat.

The other day I went to the shoe repairer to have him repair two pairs of shoes. They needed heels and soles. I stopped at the grocery store and bought a newspaper. I bought a bottle of orange juice, too.

Exercise 2 Draw lines to match the homonyms (words that sound alike). Then use the blanks to tell what each word means.

1. _____ sole   pear _____

   _____   _____

2. _____ too   hour _____

   _____   _____

3. _____ heel   soul _____

   _____   _____

4. _____ pair   heal _____

   _____   _____

5. _____ our   two _____

   _____   _____

Exercise 3   Separate each compound word into two smaller words.

    1. barbershop _____

    2. dressmaker _____

    3. drugstore _____

    4. hardware _____

    5. supermarket _____

    6. warehouse _____

    7. fireman _____

    8. policewoman _____

Exercise 4   Choose the correct synonym (word with a similar meaning) from the list below. Then use each word in a sentence. You will have twelve sentences in all.

| consists of | help | community |
| attend | pharmacy | repair |

    1. fix   _____

    2. neighborhood   _____

    3. drugstore   _____

    4. has   _____

    5. go to   _____

    6. aid   _____

Now write your sentences.

    1. _____

    2. _____

    3. _____

    4. _____

    5. _____

    6. _____

    7. _____

    8. _____

    9. _____

   10. _____

   11. _____

   12. _____

Exercise 5 Find and circle the words from the list. They may read across, down, diagonally, backward and forward. One has been done for you. Then find the twelve letters you do not use. Put them in order to spell the mystery word.

community	noses	map	business
east	south	district	butcher
tailor	grocery	police	bakery
stores	race	far	near
big	cans	sale	up
to (4)			

C	E	C	I	L	O	P	D	R	B
O	E	A	F	A	R	I	N	A	I
M	L	E	S	I	S	N	A	C	G
M	A	P	H	T	U	O	S	E	R
U	S	E	R	O	T	S	G	H	E
N	B	I	B	A	K	E	R	Y	H
I	C	N	E	A	R	S	O	R	C
T	A	I	L	O	R	H	O	O	T
Y	G	R	O	C	E	R	Y	P	U
O	D	S	S	E	N	I	S	U	B

Mystery Word: _____

Exercise 6 Make as many small words as you can from the words DEPARTMENT STORE. Use each letter only once in a word.

_____

_____

_____

_____

_____

Exercise 7   Complete this crossword puzzle.

Across

1 The opposite of *far* is _____ .

3 The abbreviation for southwest

   is _____ .

5 *E* is the abbreviation for _____ .

7 I am, you _____ .

8 _____ , greater, greatest.

9 *W* is the abbreviation for _____ .

10 You buy cake in a _____ .

13 I am, _____ are.

15 You can buy house paint in

   a _____ store.

17 The abbreviation for United States

   is _____ .

18 He _____ many questions.

19 Stores are in the town's business _____ .

Down

1 A synonym for *community* is _____ .

2 A synonym for fix is _____ .

3 A department _____ is very big.

4 The abbreviation for *avenue* is _____ .

6 A _____ is in the industrial district.

11 Don't come here. Go _____ .

12 The plural of *you* is _____ .

14 I use, she _____ .

16 The abbreviation for *department* is _____ .

18 She lives _____ 21 Spring Avenue.

Exercise 8   Unscramble the words and write them in the boxes. Put only one letter in a box. Then unscramble the circled letters to find the mystery word.

e s o h u

l o b c k

a m p

a y r b e k

p a t m n e a r t

o a l t i r

a t r f y o c

e r n a

Mystery Word: _____

Unit 2 Community Helpers

Lesson 5   **The Sanitation Department**

Exercise 1   Read these paragraphs.

Our community is very clean. The Sanitation Department is very good in our neighborhood. They pick up the garbage three times a week. They also have mechanical sweepers that come around three times a week. The people who pick up the garbage work very hard. They come around in the garbage truck in all kinds of weather.

We have a group on our block that encourages everyone to put garbage in plastic bags or in garbage cans with lids on them. We don't want litterbugs. We also collect empty plastic bottles and metal cans so that we can recycle them. It is nice to live in a clean community.

Exercise 2   Identify these pictures. Use the words below to help you.

lid   trash   garbage can   bag   litterbug   garbage truck

1. _____

2. _____

3. _____

4. _____

5. _____

6. _____

Exercise 3   Match column A and column B.

	A		**B**
____	1. pick up	a.	stop by
____	2. come around	b.	person who dirties the community
____	3. kinds	c.	container
____	4. lid	d.	cover
____	5. garbage	e.	clean with a broom
____	6. can	f.	collect
____	7. litterbug	g.	trash
____	8. sweep	h.	sorts

Exercise 4   Answer the questions with complete sentences.

1. Is your community clean?_____

   If not, what can you do to make it clean? _____

   _____

2. Who cleans the streets? _____

3. What does the Sanitation Department do to keep the neighborhood

   clean?_____

   _____

4. How many times a week does the garbage truck come around? _____

   _____

5. Is the garbage picked up when it snows? _____

6. How do we punish litterbugs? _____

   _____

Exercise 5   Make a list of rules to help keep your community clean.

1. Don't throw _____ in the street.

2. All garbage cans should have _____ on them.

3. Put bottles and cans in _____ .

4. _____ .

5. _____ .

Exercise 6   You see someone litter. What do you tell him or her? What does he or she say?

     You: _____

     Litterbug: _____

     You: _____

     Litterbug: _____

Lesson **6**   The Police Department

Exercise 1   Study the following sentences.

1. A *nice guy* is a good man.
2. The *precinct* is the district where the police from one police station work.
3. A *cheerful* person often smiles.
4. The *mounted police* ride on horses, not in cars.
5. The *patrol car* is the car that police use to go around the neighborhood and see that everything is all right.
6. *Responsibility* is what you are obligated to do. It's your duty.
7. When something is *hard* to do, it is difficult.
8. A *crime* is when you break the law.
9. *Criminals* are people who break the law.
10. *Robbers* are criminals who steal things.

Exercise 2   Match the synonyms (words with similar meanings).

	A		**B**
____	1. cheerful	a.	happy
____	2. responsibility	b.	bad act
____	3. hard	c.	thieves
____	4. guy	d.	duty
____	5. robbers	e.	man
____	6. crime	f.	difficult

Exercise 3   Read the following paragraphs.

       Officer Kelly is a nice guy. He is the police officer who helps us cross the street on the way to school. He always has a smile on his face, and always gives us a cheerful "Good morning." He works in the sixth precinct. The station is in our neighborhood. Most of the police officers are very nice. Some patrol the neighborhood in a patrol car, and some are mounted police.

       One day Officer Kelly spoke to us in our social studies class. He told us about the Police Academy and how to become a police officer. It is a hard and dangerous job. The police have many responsibilities.

Exercise 4   Complete the sentences.

1. Officer Kelly is a _____ .

2. He always has a _____ on his face.

3. He works in the _____ precinct.

4. A precinct is a _____ .

5. Some police are in a _____ and some are on _____ .

6. Officer Kelly told us _____

_____ .

7. You must attend the _____ to become a _____ .

8. A police officer has many _____ .

9. It is a _____ and _____ job.

Exercise 5   What does a police officer do? Name five things.

1. _____

2. _____

3. _____

4. _____

5. _____

Exercise 6   Interview your neighborhood police officer. Ask him or her:

1. When did you decide to become a police officer?
2. Why did you want to become a police officer?
3. What are your responsibilities?
4. What do you like about your job?
5. What don't you like about your job?
6. Describe your daily routine.

_____

_____

_____

_____

_____

_____

_____

_____

_____

_____

_____

_____

_____

_____

_____

_____

_____

_____

_____

Lesson 7 The Fire Department

Exercise 1   Identify these pictures. Use the words below to help you.

burning building   ladder   fire engine   hose
helmet   matches   fire hydrant   alarm

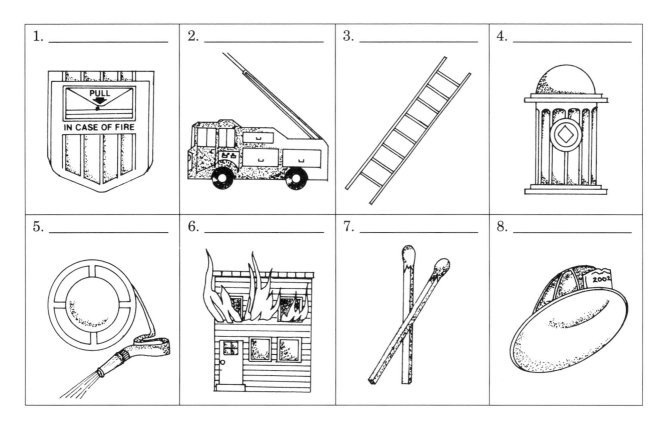

1. _____
2. _____
3. _____
4. _____
5. _____
6. _____
7. _____
8. _____

Exercise 2   Read the following paragraphs. Look carefully at the words in *italics*.

One day my friend and I visited a firehouse. The fire fighters were very nice to us. They showed us the fire engines and told us how the equipment worked. I wanted to climb the big ladder. They explained the bell system to us and told us how the fire-alarm box worked. Now we understand how *dangerous* it is when somebody rings a false alarm. We also understand how dangerous it is to play with matches.

I think fire fighters are very *brave*. They rush into burning buildings and *rescue* people who are *trapped*. They wear heavy raincoats, thick rubber boots, and helmets. They usually carry axes so that they can break windows and doors to get to the fire. It *seems like* a challenging way to earn a living.

Exercise 3   Match the synonyms.

	A		B
____	1. brave	a.	save
____	2. rescue	b.	risky
____	3. trapped	c.	functions
____	4. dangerous	d.	courageous
____	5. works	e.	caught
____	6. seems like	f.	looks like

Exercise 4   Now rewrite the paragraphs in exercise 2. Use the synonyms from exercise 3 instead of the words in italics.

_____

_____

_____

_____

_____

_____

_____

_____

_____

_____

_____

_____

_____

_____

_____

_____

_____

_____

Exercise 5   Complete the sentences.

1. I think fire fighters are very _____ .

2. They rush into _____ and

   rescue _____ who are _____ .

3. We visited the _____ .

4. We saw the _____ and other _____ .

5. We now understand why it is dangerous to ring a _____ .

6. The fire fighters wear _____ ,

   _____ , and _____ .

7. They carry _____ to _____

   _____ .

8. It's a _____ way to _____ a living.

9. It's dangerous to play with _____ .

Exercise 6   Match the antonyms (opposites).

	A		B
____	1. false	a.	fix
____	2. nice	b.	free
____	3. heavy	c.	mean
____	4. break	d.	dull
____	5. challenging	e.	true
____	6. trapped	f.	light

Exercise 7   List the locations of fire alarms in your school.

1. _____

2. _____

3. _____

4. _____

Lesson **8**   Fire Prevention

Exercise 1   Match the synonyms.

	A		B
____	1. end	a.	get to
____	2. quietly	b.	bell
____	3. rules	c.	finish
____	4. film	d.	movie
____	5. drill	e.	directions
____	6. reach	f.	silently
____	7. quickly	g.	fast
____	8. gong	h.	exercise

Exercise 2   Match the antonyms.

	A		B
____	1. end	a.	blocked
____	2. quickly	b.	disregard
____	3. quietly	c.	beginning
____	4. follow	d.	noisily
____	5. never	e.	slowly
____	6. clear	f.	always

Exercise 3   Read the following paragraphs.

Last week was Fire Prevention Week in school. The fire department sent a fire fighter to show us a film on fire safety and to talk to us at our assembly. He spoke to us about keeping the fire escape clear and easy to reach. He also mentioned the use of matches. He warned us never to leave matches where children could reach them. At the end of his talk, he invited us to visit the firehouse.

That afternoon we had a fire drill in school. As soon as the gongs sounded, our teacher led us out of the school quickly and quietly. Fire is a dangerous thing, so it is important to know and follow the rules of safety.

Exercise 4   Answer the questions with complete sentences.

1. Why must the fire escape be kept clear and easy to reach? _____

_____

2. What must you do if you smell smoke? _____

_____

3. Why must you keep matches away from children? _____

_____

4. What is a fire drill? _____

_____

5. Why is a fire drill important? _____

_____

6. Describe a fire drill in your school. _____

_____

_____

_____

7. Why must you keep quiet during a fire drill? _____

_____

8. Why must you walk quickly in a fire drill, but not run? _____

_____

9. What can you do during Fire Prevention Week? _____

_____

_____

_____

Exercise 5   Make a list of safety rules to prevent fires.

1. _____

2. _____

3. _____

4. _____

5. _____

6. _____

Lesson 9 The Postal Service

Exercise 1 Identify these pictures. Use the words below to help you.

stamp   envelope   package   letter   mailbox

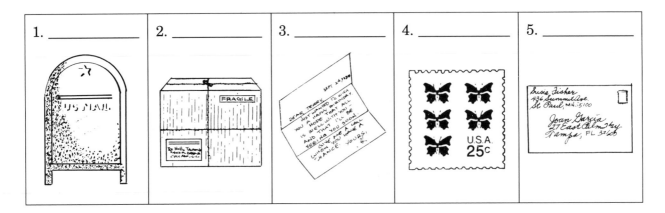

1. _____
2. _____
3. _____
4. _____
5. _____

Exercise 2 Match the synonyms. Then look for the words in column A as you read exercise 3.

A	B
____ 1. bring	a. purchase
____ 2. pleasant	b. shipped
____ 3. sent	c. carry
____ 4. pick up	d. get
____ 5. buy	e. cheerful

Exercise 3 Read the following paragraphs.

In the morning a woman in a gray uniform comes to our house to bring the mail. It doesn't matter what the weather is like. She is there every day except Sunday. Her name is Lydia and she works for the U.S. Postal Service. She is a very pleasant mail carrier. Whenever she has an important letter or package for us, she rings the bell.

She knows everybody in the neighborhood, and everyone knows her. Even the dogs know her and don't bite her. We always meet Lydia on our way to school. She always stops to talk to us.

This afternoon I have to go to the post office to pick up a package that was sent to us from Puerto Rico. Lydia doesn't deliver big packages. While I'm in the post office, I'll buy some stamps. I'll also pick up a passport application. I'll buy some envelopes, too. The post office is closed on Sunday, and the mail carrier doesn't come then either.

Exercise 4   True or false? If the sentence is false, correct it.

1. The mail carrier wears a gray uniform. _____

2. She delivers mail every day. _____

3. The mail carrier sells stamps. _____

4. She works for the federal government. _____

5. She doesn't come when it rains. _____

6. You must go to Washington for a passport. _____

7. The mail carrier doesn't deliver big packages. _____

8. There is no mail on Sunday. _____

9. The post office sells envelopes. _____

10. The post office does not have passport applications. _____

_____

Exercise 5   Match the homonyms (words that sound alike) and write a sentence for each. You will have ten sentences in all.

____	1. way	a.	meat
____	2. know	b.	no
____	3. mail	c.	weigh
____	4. meet	d.	cent
____	5. sent	e.	male

Now write your sentences.

1. _____

2. _____

3. _____

4. _____

5. _____

6. _____

7. _____

8. _____

9. _____

10. _____

Exercise 6   Unscramble the words. Then unscramble the circled letters to find a mystery word.

a l i m

▢ ▢ ▢ ◯

p t m s a

▢ ◯ ▢ ▢

r t l t e e

▢ ▢ ◯ ▢ ▢

p e n o e v l e

◯ ▢ ▢ ▢ ▢ ▢ ◯

e i r e l d v

▢ ▢ ▢ ▢ ▢ ◯

Mystery Word: _____

Lesson **10**   **A Business Letter**

Exercise 1   Read the business letter. Then study the rules that follow it.

```
                                          4709 Logan St.
                                          Los Angeles, CA 91200
                                          August 12, 1990

James Sargeant, President
Sargeant Lawn Equipment
1102 W. Grand Ave.
Chicago, IL 60600

Dear Mr. Sargeant:

   I recently bought a lawn mower made by your company.  The
salesperson told me that it was the best on the market.  After
using it for three months, I know that the salesperson was
right.
   I am very pleased with your product.  I will recommend it to
all my friends.

                                          Sincerely,

                                          Frank Griffith

                                          Frank Griffith
```

Everyday English, Book Three

Rules for a business letter:

1. In a business letter, your address and the date go in the upper right-hand corner. Don't forget the zip code.
2. The name of the person you are writing to and the address of the company begin at the left margin.
3. For your greeting, use *Dear Mr., Ms., Miss, or Mrs.* and the person's name or *Dear Sir, Dear Madam,* or *To Whom It May Concern.* Put a colon (:) at the end of the greeting.
4. Write your letter. Don't forget to indent for each new paragraph.
5. For your closing, use *Sincerely* or *Yours truly.* Put it at the right, in line with your address, and put a comma after it.
6. Sign your name.

Exercise 2   Answer the questions with complete sentences.

1. What goes in the upper right-hand corner in a business letter? _____

    _____

2. What goes on the left side? _____

    _____

3. Every state has a two-letter abbreviation. (For example, *CA* is the abbreviation for California.) What is the abbreviation for your state?

    _____

4. Every city has at least one zip code. (For example, one for Chicago is

    60600.) What is your zip code? _____

5. What greetings can you use if you're writing to a man? _____

    _____

6. What greetings can you use if you're writing to a woman? _____

    _____

7. What do you write if you don't know if you're writing to a man or a

    woman? _____

8. What closings can you use at the end of the letter? _____

    _____

9. Where do you sign your name? _____

    _____

Exercise 3   Write a business letter. Use the following information.

You see an ad in the paper for a part-time secretary. You must write c/o P.O. Box 45, New York, NY 10010. Write where you saw the ad, why you want the job, and your qualifications for the job. Ask if you may have an interview and what you must bring with you.

_____

_____

_____

_____

_____

_____

_____

_____

_____

_____

_____

_____

_____

_____

_____

_____

_____

_____

Exercise 4   Write a business letter. Use your own information.

_____

_____

_____

_____

_____

_____

_____

_____

_____

_____

_____

_____

_____

_____

_____

_____

_____

_____

Exercise 1   Read this informal letter. Then study the rules that follow it.

December 15, 1990

Dear Joan,
        I just wanted to thank you for the birthday present you sent.
        The sweater is beautiful. It's my favorite color and it's perfect for these cold winter days.
        I can't wait to wear it. Thanks again.
                                    Love,
                                    Susie

Rules for an informal letter:

1. Write the date in the upper right-hand corner.
2. Write *Dear* and the person's name on the next line on the left side. Put a comma after the name.
3. Write the message, or the body, of your letter.
4. Close your letter with words such as *Affectionately, Always, Love,* or *Regards* in line with the date. Put a comma after the closing.
5. Sign your name under the closing.

Exercise 2   Now look at the envelope. Then study the rules that follow it.

Susie Fisher
486 Summit Ave.
St. Paul, MN 55100

FIRST DAY OF ISSUE
2 16 DEC 1990
ST. PAUL
MN

U.S.A.
25c

Joan Carson
27 East Palm Way
Tampa, FL 33600

Rules for addressing an envelope:

1. Put your name and address in the upper left-hand corner of the envelope.
2. Write the name and address of the person you are writing to in the center of the envelope.
3. Put a stamp in the upper right-hand corner of the envelope.
4. For an airmail letter, write *Airmail* in the lower left-hand corner.

Exercise 3   Write a short letter to a friend and tell what you are doing in school this week.

_____

_____

_____

_____

_____

_____

_____

_____

_____

_____

_____

_____

_____

_____

_____

_____

Exercise 4   Write a letter to a friend or relative here or in your native country. Tell about your community, school, and friends.

_____

_____

_____

_____

_____

_____

_____

_____

_____

_____

_____

_____

_____

_____

Exercise 5   Address the envelope.

_____

_____

_____

_____

_____

_____

Everyday English, Book Three

Lesson 12 Review of Community Helpers

Exercise 1   Complete this crossword puzzle.

Across

1 To _____ is to clean with a broom.

4 We buy stamps in the _____ office.

6 Fire fighters use a _____ ladder to save people trapped in a burning building.

7 Sometimes people jump from a burning building into a _____ .

8 Don't be a _____ . Help keep streets clean.

11 I want to be a fire fighter _____ a police officer

13 A fire fighter _____ lives.

14 If you aren't late, you're on _____ .

16 During a _____ drill, we leave the school quickly.

17 A synonym for *garbage* is _____ .

21 Fire fighters wear heavy _____s on their feet.

22 Put your _____ in the mailbox.

23 If you are pleasant, you are _____ful.

24 Robbery and murder are _____ .

Down

1 The _____ department keeps our city clean.

2 To go in is to _____ .

3 The _____ fight crime.

5 A large machine _____ the street clean.

6 Put your garbage in a _____ or a can.

9 A synonym for *courage* is _____ .

10 The district where a policewoman works is her _____ .

12 A synonym for *responsibility* _____ *duty*.

15 Don't play with _____ . You can start a fire.

18 Don't ring a false _____ . It's dangerous.

19 A _____ protects a fire fighter's head from fire.

20 An _____ word for *trapped* is *caught*.

21 To sweep is to clean with a _____ .

23 A _____ is a kind of container.

Exercise 2   Answer the questions with complete sentences.

What do you do if:

1. you are lost? _____

_____

2. you see a fire? _____

_____

3. you see a robbery? _____

_____

4. you want to mail a letter? _____

_____

5. you throw something out? _____

_____

6. you want to mail a package? _____

_____

7. your house is robbed? _____

_____

8. your street is full of garbage? _____

_____

9. your cat is stuck in a tree? _____

_____

10. you want to buy a stamp? _____

_____

Exercise 3   Make as many words as you can from the words COMMUNITY
HELPERS.

_____

_____

_____

_____

_____

Everyday English, Book Three

Exercise 4   Visit the police station, firehouse, sanitation department, or post office near you. Be prepared to tell the class about your visit.

Exercise 5   Interview a community helper, or imagine an interview with a community helper. What would you ask? What would he or she answer?

_____

_____

_____

_____

_____

_____

_____

_____

_____

_____

_____

_____

_____

_____

_____

_____

_____

_____

_____

_____

_____

Exercise 6

Find and circle the hidden words from the list. They may read across, down, diagonally, forward, or backward. Then find the nine letters you do not use. Put them in order to spell the mystery word.

garbage can	crime	robbery
postman	mail	letter
sanitation	precincts	boots
helmets	mounted	patrol car
engine	brooms	hose
stamp	post	lid
door	oven	moon
pin		

G	S	A	N	I	T	A	T	I	O	N	L
S	A	M	O	U	N	T	E	D	O	O	R
T	S	R	O	V	E	N	G	I	N	E	A
C	T	O	B	O	I	I	E	P	T	T	C
N	E	B	R	A	N	P	M	A	I	L	L
I	M	B	O	P	G	A	I	L	H	E	O
C	L	E	O	O	T	E	R	I	O	T	R
E	E	R	M	S	T	E	C	D	S	T	T
R	H	Y	S	T	R	S	B	A	E	E	A
P	O	S	T	M	A	N	U	G	N	R	P

Mystery Word: _____

Everyday English, Book Three

Unit 3 Department Stores

Lesson 13 Different Departments

Exercise 1   Read the following dialogue.

Felix: I don't like small stores. The selection is limited and I don't like salespeople always asking me what I want.

Lan: Let's go to Jones's Department Store. No one bothers you and you can find almost anything you want. It's cheaper, too.

Felix: I have to buy pants for myself and a pot for my mother.

(At the store)

Lan: The pants are in the men's clothing department on the fifth floor. The pots and pans are on the third floor in the housewares department.

Felix: How do you know that?

Lan: I come to Jones's often. My cousin, Hong, is the manager.

Felix: Does she give you a discount?

Lan: No, I pay the same price as everyone else. By the way, if the pot is a gift, you can have it wrapped up at the service counter on the sixth floor.

Felix: That's a good idea. I'll have to come here more often.

Exercise 2   Complete the sentences.

1. The selection in a small store is _____ .

2. A department store is good because _____

_____ .

3. Pants are in the _____ department.

4. Pots and pans are in the _____ department.

5. The _____ will wrap up your gift.

37

Exercise 3   Circle the words that best complete the sentences.

1. A store department is _____ .

   a. an apartment   b. a section   c. a store

2. A synonym for *floor* is _____ .

   a. level   b. section   c. wall

3. A clerk is a _____ .

   a. customer   b. manager   c. salesperson

4. A manager is the _____ .

   a. chief   b. salesperson   c. cashier

5. If you bother people, you _____ them.

   a. like   b. annoy   c. hit

6. A gift is a _____ .

   a. dress   b. give   c. present

7. To wrap up is to _____ .

   a. get dressed   b. make a package   c. send

8. If something is cheap, _____ .

   a. it doesn't cost much   b. it's expensive   c. it's good

9. A discount is a _____ .

   a. mistake   b. store   c. lower price

10. A shopping mall is a _____ .

    a. center with many stores   b. hall   c. store

Exercise 4   Match each picture with the store department it comes from.

a. Service counter   d. Book section

b. Sports department   e. Housewares

c. Men's clothing department

1. _____	2. _____	3. _____	4. _____	5. _____

Exercise 5   Complete the dialogue.

Your friend: Let's go shopping.

You: _____

_____

Your friend: No, let's go to a department store.

You: _____

_____

Your friend: Because there's a bigger selection.

You: _____

_____

Your friend: Don't worry. We'll be back by 5:00.

Lesson 14 Getting Around

Exercise 1   Discuss the picture of a department store.

Exercise 2   Read the following paragraph. Refer to the picture as you read.

This is the ground floor of a department store. Below the sign "Ground Floor" is the men's department. The information desk is to the left of the men's department. To the right is the glove and scarf counter. There is a sale. There are gloves on the counter and in the display case. There are two customers next to the counter. The salesperson is behind the counter. Behind the counter is the fitting room for the lingerie section. Can you find the escalator and the elevator to take you to the other floors? What department is the escalator in front of?

Exercise 3   Match the words in column A and column B to make complete sentences.

A	B
____ 1. A moving stairway is an	a. merchandise is displayed.
____ 2. An _____ carries you from	b. *in back of.*
floor to floor.	c. information desk.

Everyday English, Book Three

_____ 3. You can get help at an   d. what you sell or buy.

_____ 4. A customer is a   e. client.

_____ 5. The counter is where   f. in the display case.

_____ 6. A sale is when   g. clerk.

_____ 7. A synonym for _behind_ is   h. elevator.

_____ 8. A synonym for _in front of_ are   i. on the counter.

_____ 9. Some merchandise is   j. _ahead of_ and _before._

_____ 10. Some merchandise is   k. prices are lowered.

_____ 11. A salesperson is a   l. escalator.

_____ 12. Merchandise is

Exercise 4   There is one mistake in each sentence. Find it and cross it out. Then find a word or words from the list to make the sentence correct. Write the word on the blank.

below	department	sale
elevator	escalator	counter
salesperson	information desk	customer
fitting rooms		

1. This is the ground floor of a small store. _____

2. Over the sign "Ground Floor" is the men's department. _____

3. The men's room is to the left of the men's department. _____

4. At the left of the picture is the elevator. _____

5. There is a discount. _____

6. There are gloves on the floor. _____

7. The customer is behind the counter. _____

8. Behind the counter is a display case for the lingerie. _____

9. The stairs or the elevator will take you to the other floors. _____

10. The display case wants to buy some gloves. _____

Exercise 5   Look in the newspaper for two ads for two different department stores. Then answer these questions.

What are the names of the department stores? _____

_____

Where are they located? _____

_____

What is on sale? _____

How long will the sale last? _____

What is the regular price? What is the sale price? _____

_____

Are the prices high or low? _____

_____

Any other information? _____

_____

_____

Lesson **15** Buying Clothes

Exercise 1   Study the following vocabulary.

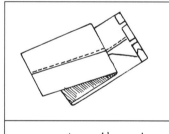

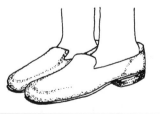

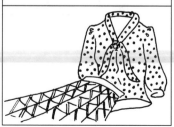

1. How much is that *pair* of pants?

2. These shoes don't *fit*. They're too big.

3. The blouse and skirt don't *match*.

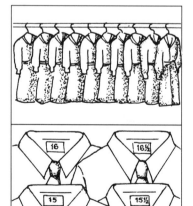

4. Let's look at that *rack* of dresses.

5. They have only four *sizes*.

Everyday English, Book Three

Exercise 2   Read the following dialogue.

Anna: I need some new clothes. Let's go shopping.

Tanya: OK. Where do you want to go?

Anna: Let's go to Jones's Department Store. Their prices are low.

(At the store)

Salesperson: May I help you?

Anna: Yes, I would like a skirt and a blouse to match.

Salesperson: What size do you wear?

Anna: I wear a size-eight skirt and a size-eight or -ten blouse.

Salesperson: Here's the size-eight rack.

(In the fitting room)

Tanya: How do they fit, Anna?

Anna: I think they're OK. What do you think?

Tanya: They fit very well. They look nice.

Anna: They're not very expensive. I'll take both, the skirt and the blouse. I'll be able to buy a pair of shoes, too.

(At the counter)

Salesperson: Did you find anything?

Anna: Yes, I'll take this skirt and blouse.

Salesperson: That'll be thirty-five dollars. please.

Anna: I'd like to buy a pair of shoes, too. Where is the shoe department?

Salesperson: On the third floor.

Tanya and Anna: Thank you.

Exercise 3   Complete the dialogue.

Salesperson: May I help you?

You: _____

_____

Salesperson: What size do you wear?

You: _____

_____

Salesperson: What color do you want?

You: _____

Salesperson: How does it fit?

You: _____

Salesperson: Would you like anything else?

You: _____

_____

Salesperson: That will be _____ dollars. Pay the cashier, please.

You: _____

Exercise 4   Make your own ad for a sale on coats.

Lesson 16 Buying a Television

Exercise 1   Match column A and column B.

	A		B
____	1. make	a.	famous
____	2. well-known	b.	work
____	3. portable	c.	want to spend
____	4. afford	d.	brand
____	5. operate	e.	can be carried

Exercise 2   Look at the synonyms in Exercise 1. Then read the dialogue. Look closely at the words in italics.

Mr. Yuan: I'd like to buy a television set.

Salesperson: TV sets are on the fourth floor. Take the elevator to the left.

(On the fourth floor)

Salesperson: May I help you?

Mr. Yuan: Yes, I'd like to buy a television set.

Salesperson: Are you interested in any particular set?

Mr. Yuan: Yes, I'd like a *well-known make*; a *portable* black-and-white.

Salesperson: We carry all the well-known makes.

Mr. Yuan: I want a set in the price range of $300.

Salesperson: For about $300, you can get a nice, black-and-white, table-model set.

Mr. Yuan: What about a color set?

Salesperson: A color set costs about $450.

Mr. Yuan: That's more than I can *afford*. What size screen does the *portable* set over there have?

Salesperson: That's a sixteen-inch screen. It costs only $225.

Mr. Yuan: Could you please turn it on for me? I'd like to see how it works.

Salesperson: Certainly. The picture is very clear, and it's very easy to *operate*. You just turn this dial, and the picture comes on immediately.

Mr. Yuan:	I'll take it.
Salesperson:	Fine, sir. If you're not satisfied, we'll exchange it for you within seven days. Please pay the cashier.
Mr. Yuan:	Thank you.

Exercise 3   Study the parts of a television.

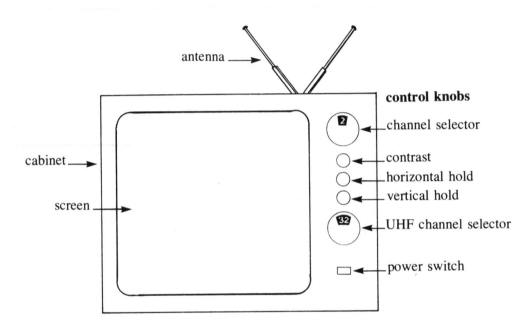

Exercise 4   Match column A and column B.

	A		**B**
____	1. screen	a.	station
____	2. cabinet	b.	helps give a clear picture
____	3. antenna	c.	gives you ultra-high-frequency channels
____	4. knobs	d.	where you watch the picture
____	5. horizontal hold	e.	turns the TV on and off
____	6. vertical hold	f.	holds the TV together
____	7. contrast	g.	changes channels
____	8. UHF	h.	adjust the TV
____	9. power switch	i.	adjusts the light and dark
____	10. channel selector	j.	adjusts the picture horizontally (across)
____	11. channel	k.	adjusts the picture vertically (up and down)

Everyday English, Book Three

Lesson **17** Review of Department Stores

Exercise 1 Find brand names for these items. Look in newspapers or magazines if you need help.

1. shirts _____

2. women's blouses _____

3. stockings _____

4. bicycles _____

5. television sets _____

6. radios _____

7. beds _____

8. dishes _____

9. tissues _____

10. refrigerators _____

11. gym shoes _____

12. other things _____

_____

_____

_____

_____

_____

_____

Exercise 2 Answer these questions.

1. How many channels do you get on your TV?

_____

2. What is your favorite channel?

_____

3. What is your favorite program?

_____

4. When is it on TV?

_____

5. What make is your TV?

_____

6. Is it a color set or a black-and-white set?

_____

7. What size is your TV screen?

_____

8. What is cable TV?

_____

Exercise 3 Give an example of each type of TV show.

1. movie _____

2. game show _____

3. comedy _____

4. educational program _____

5. soap opera _____

6. news broadcast _____

7. children's program _____

8. special _____

9. late show _____

10. talk show _____

11. sports show _____

12. commercial _____

Exercise 4   Do you think watching a lot of television is good or bad? Why?

_____

_____

_____

_____

_____

_____

_____

_____

_____

_____

_____

_____

_____

_____

_____

_____

_____

_____

_____

_____

_____

_____

Unit 4 Small Stores

Lesson 18 The Bakery

Exercise 1   Identify these pictures. Use the words below to help you.

cookies   bakery   muffin   doughnut   pie   pound

pastry   snack   sliced   loaf of bread   cake   ounce

1. _____

2. _____

3. _____

4. _____

5. _____

6. _____

7. _____

8. _____

9. _____

10. _____

11. _____

12. _____

Exercise 2   Read the dialogue. The words in italics can be replaced.

Claude: I'm hungry. Let's have a snack. What would you like?

Peter: I'd like some pastry. Let's go to the bakery.

Claude: Mmmmmmm. That's a good idea.

(At the bakery)

Baker: May I help you? These *cookies* are delicious.

Claude: I'd like a *strawberry tart* and a *jelly doughnut*, please.

Peter: I'll take a *pound of chocolate chip cookies* and a *blueberry muffin.*

Baker: Is there anything else?

Claude: No, thank you.

Peter: Oh, I almost forgot, my father wants me to buy a *sliced loaf of rye bread.*

Baker: That will be $5.50 altogether.

Peter: I'll pay, Claude, and then you give me what you owe me. I have the money ready.

Claude: OK. Now let's go get something to drink.

Exercise 3   Answer the questions with complete sentences.

1. Where can you buy bread, cake, and cookies?

    _____

2. What does Peter want to buy?

    _____

3. What does Claude ask for?

    _____

4. What does Peter ask for?

    _____

Lesson **19** The Barbershop

Exercise 1   Match the words with their definitions.

	A		**B**
____	1. barber	a.	a blade used to shave faces
____	2. smock	b.	cut just a little bit
____	3. razor	c.	a person who cuts men's hair
____	4. trim	d.	clean, shape, and polish nails
____	5. manicure	e.	a big apron that protects your clothing

Exercise 2   Read the following dialogue. Look for the vocabulary from exercise 1.

Seth: I think I'll go for a haircut. My hair is getting much too long.

Sharon: Oh, leave it long. I like it that way.

Seth: I'll just have it cut a little bit. Come with me to the barbershop.

Sharon: OK.

(At the barber shop)

Barber: May I help you?

Seth: Yes, I'd like a trim, please. Leave my hair as long as you can.

Barber: Sit down, lean back, and relax. Let me tie this smock around your neck so the hair won't fall all over you. Would you like a shave and a manicure.

Seth: No, thanks; just a trim.

(Later)

Sharon: Wow! The barber did a great job. You really look good — so good that you should let everyone see you. How about taking me to the school party tonight?

Seth: OK. I'll pick you up at 8:00.

Exercise 3   There is a wrong word in each sentence. Find the word and correct it so that the sentence makes sense.

1. Seth wants to go for a hairpiece. _____

2. His hare is too long. _____

3. Sharon likes Seth's hair wrong. _____

4. Seth likes to go to the barber show. _____

5. He wants a brim only. _____

6. The robber tells Seth to relax. _____

7. He ties a smack around Seth's neck. _____

8. Seth doesn't want a shape. _____

9. Sharon thought Seth's hair rooked good. _____

10. They went to the school pantry that night. _____

Exercise 4   Unscramble the following words. Then use each one in a sentence.

1. m k s o c _____   _____

                                      _____

                                      _____

2. a r h i _____   _____

                                      _____

                                      _____

3. m i r t _____   _____

                                      _____

                                      _____

4. b a e b r r _____   _____

                                      _____

                                      _____

5. a i c e m n u r _____   _____

_____   _____

                                      _____

Lesson 20 The Hairdresser's

Exercise 1   Study the following vocabulary.

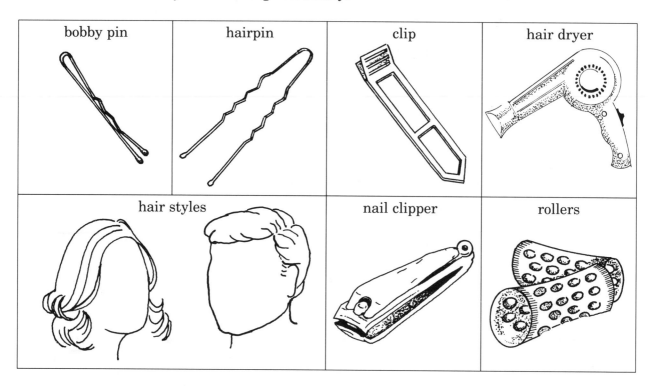

| bobby pin | hairpin | clip | hair dryer |
| hair styles | | nail clipper | rollers |

Exercise 2   Read the paragraph. Look for the vocabulary from exercise 1.

Many women and men go to the hairdresser's. They like to have their hair cut and styled. First they put on a smock to protect their clothing. Then an assistant washes their hair. A stylist cuts their hair and styles it. Men and women can also have manicures. A manicurist shapes their nails and puts on clear or colored polish. When the customer is ready to leave, they usually tip the assistant, the manicurist, and the stylist.

Exercise 3   Complete the dialogue.

Stylist: Hello, Mrs. Kern. Have a seat.

Mrs. Kern: _____ .

Stylist: What would you like today?

Mrs. Kern: _____ .

Stylist: How much do you want to have cut?

Mrs. Kern: _____ .

Stylist: The assistant will wash your hair, and then I'll cut and style it.

Mrs. Kern: _____ .

(Later)

Mrs. Kern: You did a great job. Can I make my next appointment for April 15 at 4:00?

Stylist: _____ .

Mrs. Kern: That will be perfect. See you next month.

Exercise 4   Match column A and column B.

A	B
_____ 1. hairpin	a. used to set hair
_____ 2. nail clippers	b. used to dry hair
_____ 3. rollers	c. used to trim nails
_____ 4. manicure	d. used to keep hair in place
_____ 5. hair dryer	e. to shape and polish nails

Exercise 5   Complete the sentences.

1. The person who cuts hair at a hairdresser's is a _____ .

2. People go to a hairdresser's to _____ .

3. Customers usually give a _____ to the manicurist and the stylist.

4. People wear a _____ while their hair is being cut.

Lesson 21 The Butcher's Shop

Exercise 1 Identify these pictures. Use the words below to help you.

butcher	chicken	steak
bone	bacon	sausage
hamburger	ham	frankfurter (hot dog)

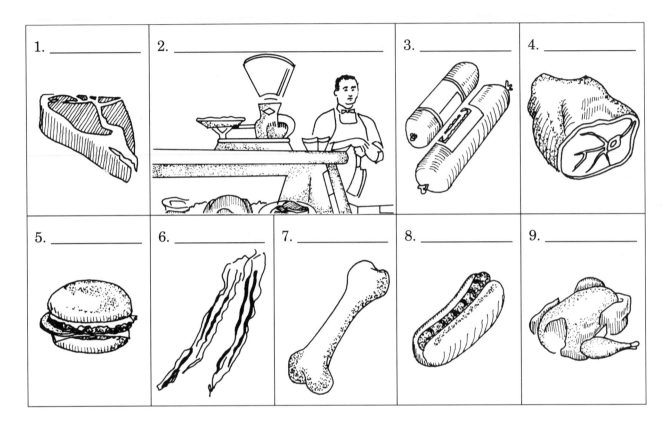

1. _____
2. _____
3. _____
4. _____
5. _____
6. _____
7. _____
8. _____
9. _____

Exercise 2 Study the following sentences.

1. *Ground beef* is the meat we use to make hamburgers.

2. *Beef* is meat from a cow.

3. *Steak* is a kind of beef.

4. *Liver* is very lean and contains a lot of iron.

5. *Pork* is meat from a pig.

6. *Ham* is smoked pork.

7. *Spareribs* are the side bones of a pig with the meat on them.

8. *Fat* is the white part of the meat. It's greasy.

9. *Lean* meat has almost no fat.

Exercise 3   Read the dialogue. (You can change the words in italics.)

Butcher: May I help you?

Maria: May I please have a *half-pound of ground beef, two steaks, and a large chicken?*

Butcher: Do you want me to cut off the fat?

Maria: *Yes, please; too much fat isn't good for you.*

Butcher: Maybe not, but it gives the meat a good taste. I'll cut it off for you if that's what you want.

Maria: Can I have some *soup bones?*

Butcher: Will there be anything else? The *liver* is fresh today.

Maria: No, thanks, that'll be all.

Butcher: *$21.00,* please.

Maria: Here you are. Good-bye.

Exercise 4   Answer the questions with complete sentences.

1. What does Maria want? _____

_____

2. Does the butcher cut off the fat? _____

_____

3. Why does Maria want soup bones? _____

_____

4. What is fresh today? _____

_____

5. How much does Maria's meat cost?_____

_____

Exercise 5   Rewrite the dialogue. Change all the words or phrases in italics.

_____

_____

_____

_____

_____

_____

_____

_____

_____

_____

_____

_____

_____

_____

_____

Exercise 6   Find an ad for meat in the newspaper. Then answer the questions.

1. Who is advertising? _____

_____

2. What is the ad advertising?_____

_____

3. How much is the meat? _____

_____

4. Where is the store? _____

_____

5. Is it a butcher's shop or a supermarket? _____

_____

Everyday English, Book Three

Lesson 22 The Fish Market

Exercise 1   Study the following vocabulary.

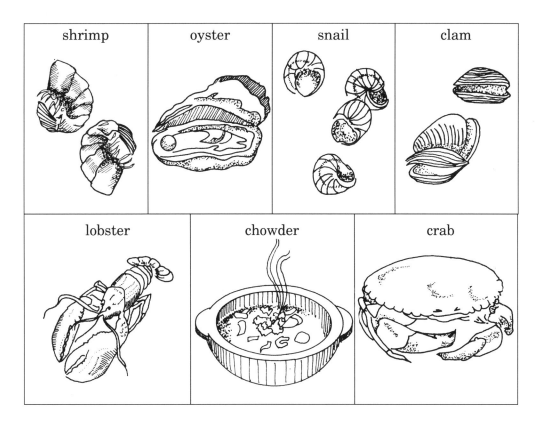

shrimp	oyster	snail	clam
lobster	chowder	crab	

Study the following vocabulary.

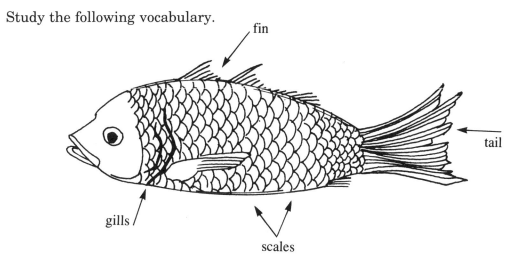

Study the names of different types of fish: shrimp, cod, flounder, tuna, salmon, trout.

Exercise 2   Match the words with their definitions.

	A		B
____	1. filet	a.	cooked in the oven
____	2. baked	b.	cooked in a frying pan
____	3. broiled	c.	cooked in a pot with water
____	4. boiled	d.	without bones
____	5. fried	e.	cooked on a fire
____	6. chowder	f.	fish and shellfish
____	7. seafood	g.	seafood soup

Exercise 3   Read the dialogue. Underline the vocabulary from exercises 1 and 2.

Greta: I'm in the mood for seafood tonight.

Ben: I don't want to see food. I want to eat food.

Greta: Silly, I said "seafood," not "see food." Come to the fish market with me.

(At the fish market)

Clerk: Can I help you?.

Greta: Yes, please. I'd like three flounder filets and four dollars worth of shrimp. *(To Ben)* See the crabs, lobsters, shrimp, snails, and oysters? They're called shellfish because they come from the sea and have a shell, but they aren't really fish at all. Fish have fins and sometimes they have scales.

Clerk: Anything else?

Greta: No, thank you.

Clerk: That will be $8.50.

Greta: Here you are, sir. Thank you.

Clerk: Thank you. Come again.

Greta: Well, Ben, how do you want your fish? Baked, broiled, or boiled?

Ben: However you like it.

Greta: OK. Let's go.

Exercise 4   How many kinds of seafood can you recognize in the fish market?

1. _____

2. _____

3. _____

4. _____

5. _____

6. _____

7. _____

8. _____

9. _____

10. _____

Exercise 5   Answer the questions with complete sentences.

1. What is your favorite shellfish? _____

_____

2. What is your favorite fish? _____

_____

3. How do you like your fish — baked, broiled, boiled, or fried?

_____

_____

4. Why are lobster and shrimp called shellfish?_____

_____

5. What is chowder?_____

Lesson 23 The Hardware Store

Exercise 1   Identify the pictures. Use the words below to help you.

hammer   nails   rope   wallpaper   screws
tape   shelves   stepladder brackets   curtain rod

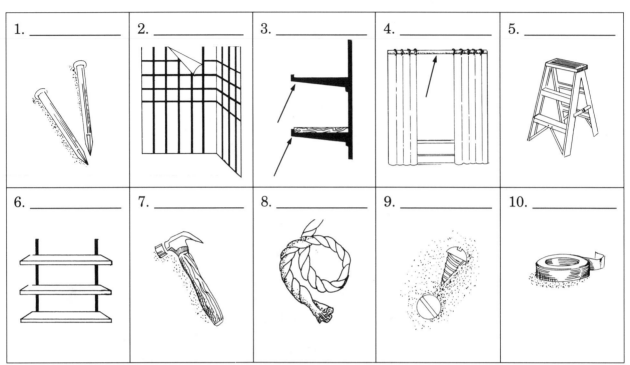

1. _____   2. _____   3. _____   4. _____   5. _____

6. _____   7. _____   8. _____   9. _____   10. _____

Exercise 2   Read the dialogue. Refer to the vocabulary from exercise 1.

Toshiko: The house is falling apart. The curtain rod is broken, the bookshelves are coming off the wall, the bedroom light doesn't work, and the wallpaper in the bathroom is torn.

Eric: Why don't you go to the hardware store and buy what you need to fix everything? I'll go with you.

Toshiko: That's a good idea.

(At the hardware store)

Salesman: Can I help you?

Toshiko: I'd like a hammer, a box of nails, a box of screws, a curtain rod, wallpaper and paste, brackets, a 100-watt bulb, and lots of help.

Salesman: Are you building a house or something?

Eric: Toshiko, look at all these kitchen gadgets.

Toshiko: Not now. We have work to do.

Salesman: That will be $45.00 even.

Toshiko: Here you are.

Salesman: Thank you. Come again.

Exercise 3   Answer the questions with complete sentences.

1. What's wrong with the house? _____

_____

_____

_____

2. What does Eric suggest? _____

_____

3. What does Toshiko buy?_____

_____

4. What does Eric want to look at?_____

_____

5. How much does everything cost? _____

_____

6. Who fixes things in your home? _____

_____

Exercise 4   One word in each sentence is wrong. Rewrite the sentences correctly.

1. The house is falling down. _____

2. The curtain red is broken. _____

3. The bedroom white doesn't work. _____

_____

4. Toshiko goes to the department store to buy everything he needs.

_____

_____

5. That will be $45.00 ever. _____

Lesson **24** The Tailor's Shop

Exercise 1   Identify the pictures. Use the words below to help you.

pin   needle   thread   cuff   hem   seam

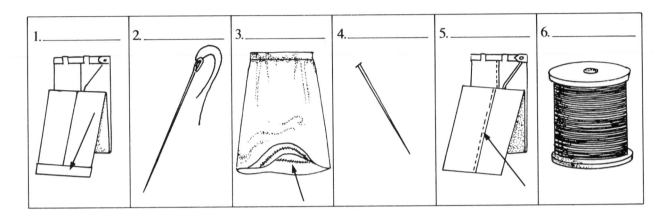

1. _____   2. _____   3. _____   4. _____   5. _____   6. _____

Exercise 2   Match the words in column A with the definitions in column B.

A	B
_____ 1. hem	a. make smaller
_____ 2. seam	b. edge sewed at the bottom of a skirt
_____ 3. cuff	c. small pointed piece of metal
_____ 4. take in	d. cloth
_____ 5. let out	e. loop made with a needle and thread
_____ 6. pin	f. fold at the bottom of a sleeve or pants leg
_____ 7. stitch	g. where two pieces of material are joined
_____ 8. material	h. make bigger

Exercise 3   Read the dialogue. Refer to the vocabulary in exercise 1.

Al: I can't zip up these pants. I didn't think I had gained so much weight. They're also a little too long.

Pak: Look, this skirt is too big on me. You gained the weight I lost.

Al: We'll take them to the tailor tomorrow.

(The next day at the tailor's shop)

Tailor: What can I do for you?

Pak: We'd like some alterations on these clothes. Al's pants have to be let out and shortened. My skirt has to be taken in at the waist and shortened.

Tailor: Step into the fitting room, please.

Al: *(Puts on the pants)* What do you think?

Tailor: I can let out an inch in the seam. Do you want cuffs on your pants or plain bottoms?

Al: No, I like cuffs.

Tailor: Let me pin them up for you.

Pak: How about my skirt?

Tailor: I'll take in half an inch on each side, raise the hem an inch, and your skirt will fit perfectly.

Al: When will the clothes be ready?

Tailor: Will next Thursday be OK?

Pak: That'll be fine. We'll pay when we pick them up. See you next week.

Tailor: See you next week. By the way, your pants are ripped in the back. I'll sew them up right away. Remember, a stitch in time saves nine.

Exercise 4 Write a sentence with each word.

1. cuff _____

_____

2. cough_____

_____

3. seam _____

_____

4. seem _____

_____

5. pin _____

_____

6. pen _____

_____

7. hem _____

_____

8. ham _____

_____

9. stitch _____

_____

10. stick _____

_____

Exercise 5   Finish the word. Refer to the vocabulary in exercise 2.

1.   __ t i __ __ __

2.   __ i __

3.   __ __ f __

4.   __ e a __

5.   __ __ m

Exercise 6   In exercise 3, the tailor said, "A stitch in time saves nine." What does this saying mean?

_____

_____

_____

_____

_____

Do you have a saying in your native language that is the same or similar?

_____

_____

Lesson **25** **Review of Small Stores**

Exercise 1   Where do you go:

1. to buy bread?_____

2. to buy shrimp? _____

3. to buy steak? _____

4. to buy nails? _____

5. to fix a skirt?_____

6. to change your hair style? _____

7. to buy cookies? _____

8. to buy clothes? _____

Exercise 2   Match the words from column A and column B.

A	**B**
_____ 1. fin	a. hardware store
_____ 2. rye	b. skirt
_____ 3. roller	c. fish
_____ 4. shell	d. bakery
_____ 5. hem	e. nails
_____ 6. fitting room	f. butcher's shop
_____ 7. ground beef	g. clothing store
_____ 8. curtain rod	h. bread
_____ 9. cookies	i. hair style
_____ 10. manicure	j. crab

Exercise 3   Find and circle the hidden words from the list. They may read across, down, diagonally, forward, or backward. Then find the six letters you do not use. Put them in order to find the mystery word.

shrimp
clams
material
hammer
hardware
cooks
can
cake
baked
nails
fried
tuna
fat
shave

screws
wash
shape
beef
bike
neck
list
hat
ask (2)
bow
are (2)
sash
fish

H	A	R	D	W	A	R	E	N	M
S	H	R	I	M	P	S	A	T	A
I	A	T	U	N	A	I	F	A	T
F	M	O	S	C	L	A	M	S	E
R	M	E	A	S	O	T	A	H	R
D	E	N	S	C	H	O	S	S	I
E	R	E	H	R	A	A	K	I	A
K	R	C	A	E	W	K	P	S	L
A	S	K	V	W	O	B	E	E	F
B	I	K	E	S	F	R	I	E	D

Mystery Word: _____

Exercise 4   Unscramble the words. Then unscramble the circled letters to find the mystery word.

g e s a u a s

p h i s r m

m e h

e o k i c o s

n k h c c i e

i p n

Mystery Word: _____

Exercise 5

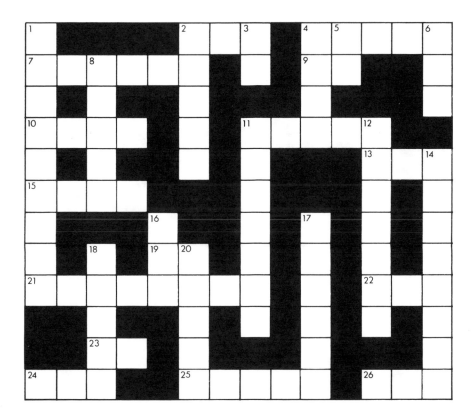

Across

2 A _____ says bow-wow.

4 _____ has a lot of iron.

7 You hit nails with a _____ .

9 The hats are _____ the counter.

10 I _____ ice cream.

11 The bottoms of your sleeves are
   called _____ .

13 _____ is smoked pork.

15 _____ have fins and scales.

19 We wear rings _____ our fingers.

21 We buy screws in a _____ store.

22 You can wear an earring in
   your _____ .

23 I read about the sale in
   an _____ in the paper.

24 _____ is a type of fish.

25 When there are _____ , prices
   are lower.

26 We fry foods in _____ .

Down

1 Lobsters and clams are both _____ .

2 People use a _____ when their hair is wet.

3 I like to _____ shopping.

4 Buy me a _____ of bread.

5 Muffins are found _____ a bakery.

6 A curtain _____ holds up the curtains.

8 A tailor _____ alterations.

11 Which do you like, cake or _____ ?

12 The plural of shelf is _____ .

14 Another word for cloth is _____ .

16 Beef is meat from a _____ .

17 We buy _____ and nails in a hardware store.

18 I like white _____ better than rye.

20 Hammer some _____ in the wall to hang up
   the pictures.

Exercise 6   Can you name a type of meat for each letter of the word *meat*?

    __ __ M

    __ E __ __

    __ A __ __ __

    __ T __ __ __

Exercise 7   Here is a list of what I bought at the fish market. What kind of fish did I buy?

    __ L __ __ __ __ __ __

    __ __ __ I __ __

    S __ __ __ __ __

    T __ __ __

Unit 5 Food

Lesson 26 Food Groups

Exercise 1   Study the following sentences.

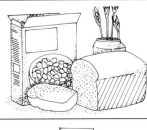

1. There are four basic food groups.

2. One group consists of *meat, seafood, poultry,* and *eggs.* (Examples of poultry are chicken and turkey.)

3. Another group is made up of *dairy products.* This group includes milk, cream, cheese, butter, ice cream, and yogurt.

4. Another consists of *fruits* and *vegetables.* (Examples of fruits are apples and oranges. Examples of vegetables are beans and carrots.)

5. The last group is made up of *bread* and *cereal.*

6. Tea, coffee, milk, and juice are *beverages.*

Exercise 2   Place the foods from the list beneath the names of the groups they belong to.

pineapple, tuna, milk, cheese, celery, cake, codfish, peach, cookie, potato, strawberry, yogurt, bread, ground beef, sausage, ham, lobster, juice, ice cream, watermelon, carrot, water, pot roast, salmon, muffin, orange, bacon, butter, clam, onion, grape, peas, mushroom, apple, oyster, chocolate milk, lettuce, oatmeal, pear, banana, corn

meat	seafood	fruit	vegetable
_____	_____	_____	_____
_____	_____	_____	_____
_____	_____	_____	_____
_____	_____	_____	_____
_____	_____	_____	_____
_____	_____	_____	_____
_____	_____	_____	_____
_____	_____	_____	_____
_____	_____	_____	_____

dairy product	bread and cereal	beverage
_____	_____	_____
_____	_____	_____
_____	_____	_____
_____	_____	_____
_____	_____	_____
_____	_____	_____
_____	_____	_____
_____	_____	_____

Exercise 3   Identify these pictures. Use vocabulary from exercise 2 and from earlier lessons.

1. _____	2. _____	3. _____	4. _____	5. _____
6. _____	7. _____	8. _____	9. _____	10. _____
11. _____	12. _____	13. _____	14. _____	15. _____
16. _____	17. _____	18. _____	19. _____	20. _____
21. _____	22. _____	23. _____	24. _____	25. _____
26. _____	27. _____	28. _____	29. _____	30. _____
31. _____	32. _____	33. _____	34. _____	35. _____

Unit 5   Food   73

Exercise 4   Unscramble these names of fruiits and vegetables. Look through
magazines and newspapers and find a picture for each one.

1. g e r a n o	2. y e r e l c	3. p e l p a
4. a r e p	5. t r o c r a	6. i n o n o
7. o t t o p a	8. n a t m o l e r e w	9. n a a a b n
10. r a g e p	11. h c a e p	12. t e e c u l t
13. p l a n p i p e e	14. u s o o r h m m	15. t o o t a m

Everyday English, Book Three

Lesson **27** Three Meals a Day

Exercise 1 Match the synonyms.

A	B
____ 1. also	a. vigorous
____ 2. hamburger	b. supper
____ 3. french fries	c. largest
____ 4. dinner	d. too
____ 5. biggest	e. fried potatoes
____ 6. strong	f. well
____ 7. healthy	g. ground beef

Exercise 2 Match the antonyms.

A	B
____ 1. first	a. morning
____ 2. can	b. few
____ 3. children	c. sick
____ 4. give	d. last
____ 5. many	e. smallest
____ 6. healthy	f. can't
____ 7. biggest	g. adults
____ 8. evening	h. night
____ 9. strong	i. take
____ 10. good	j. weak
____ 11. day	k. bad

Exercise 3   Read the following paragraphs.

Breakfast is the first meal of the day. We have juice, toast with butter, eggs, and milk. We can also have cereal.

We eat lunch at noon. Some people like to eat hamburgers and french fries. Others like tuna fish or egg salad sandwiches. Many parents give their children peanut butter and jelly sandwiches for lunch.

In the United States, dinner (supper) is usually the biggest meal of the day. We usually eat dinner at 6:00 in the evening. A large dinner may consist of soup, salad, meat or fish, vegetables, potatoes, dessert, and coffee, tea, or milk.

It is important to eat three good meals a day. That way we can be strong and healthy.

Exercise 4   Answer the questions with complete sentences.

1. Which is the first meal of the day? _____

2. What do we usually have for breakfast? _____

    _____

3. What do some people like to eat for lunch? _____

    _____

4. What do others like to eat? _____

    _____

5. What do many parents give their children for lunch?_____

    _____

6. Which is usually the biggest meal of the day? _____

    _____

7. When do we eat dinner? _____

8. What do we eat for dinner? _____

    _____

9. How many meals do we eat a day? _____

    _____

10. Why is it important to eat three good meals a day? _____

    _____

Exercise 5   Make a list of what you eat for breakfast, lunch, and dinner.

Breakfast   **Lunch**   **Dinner**

_____   _____   _____

_____   _____   _____

_____   _____   _____

_____   _____   _____

_____   _____   _____

_____   _____   _____

_____   _____   _____

_____   _____   _____

Exercise 6   Identify the pictures.

1. _____

2. _____

3. _____

4. _____

5. _____

6. _____

7. _____

8. _____

9. _____

Lesson 28 The Supermarket

Exercise 1   Look at the picture of a supermarket.

Exercise 2   Read the following paragraph.

A supermarket is a large grocery store. There are only a few people there to help you. Sometimes there is a clerk at the meat counter and in the fruit and vegetable section. People walk up and down the aisles pushing shopping carts. They choose their groceries and put them in the cart. All kinds of groceries and paper goods are sold in a supermarket. There are special counters for frozen foods, fruits and vegetables, and dairy products. There are often sales. If tomato paste usually costs 35 cents a can, on sale it may cost 65 cents for two cans. In general, food in the supermarket is cheaper than it is in a small store.

Exercise 3   Answer the questions with complete sentences.

1. What kind of store is a supermarket?_____

_____

2. Where can you find a clerk? _____

_____

3. Name three special counters in a supermarket. _____

_____

Everyday English, Book Three

4. What are five things you can buy in a supermarket? _____

   _____

5. Where do you put your groceries so you don't have to carry them?

   _____

   _____

6. Why are sales helpful? _____

   _____

Exercise 4   Solve these problems.

1. Three boxes of cookies at 79 cents each = _____

2. Four boxes of detergent at 90 cents each = _____

3. Two cans of canned pears at 60 cents each = _____

4. Five bars of soap at 45 cents each = _____

5. Three bags of sugar at $1.89 cents each = _____

Exercise 5   Look at the prices of the following grocery items:

coffee	$2.49	milk	$ .96
tuna fish	$ .85	bread	$ .85
flour	$1.29	cheese	$1.69
tea	$1.10	butter	$1.56
oranges	4 for $1.00	sugar	$1.89

Now figure out the bill for these shopping lists. Tell how much change you get.

a) 1 can of coffee   _____

   2 cans of tuna fish   _____

   16 oranges   _____

   1 bag of sugar   _____

   1 box of tea   _____

            Total   _____

   Change from $20.00   _____

b) 3 boxes of tea _____

butter _____

2 cartons of milk _____

1 bag of flour _____

4 oranges _____

Total _____

Change from $10.00 _____

c) 1 loaf of bread _____

2 packages of cheese _____

butter _____

Total _____

Change from $10.00 _____

Lesson **29** Fruit

Exercise 1   Read the following paragraphs.

There are many different kinds of fruit. Some fruits grow on trees, some on vines, and some on bushes. Most fruits have seeds. If you plant a seed, a new plant will grow from it. Pears, apples, bananas, lemons, pineapples, grapefruits, cherries, oranges, peaches, watermelons, and strawberries are fruits.

When you buy fruit, don't pick pieces that are too ripe, or not ripe enough. Don't buy damaged fruit. If you buy fruit that is in season, it will be cheaper. For example, watermelon in winter is very expensive. Many fruits and vegetables spoil very quickly, so don't buy more than you need. Keep them in the vegetable bin in your refrigerator. Don't squeeze the fruit because you will damage it.

Exercise 2   Match the words with their definitions

A	B
____ 1. ripe	a. hurt, injured
____ 2. damaged	b. become rotten
____ 3. spoil	c. ready to eat
____ 4. squeeze	d. diagram
____ 5. chart	e. hold tightly

Everyday English, Book Three

Exercise 3   Study the fruit chart and then answer the questions. "X" means "in season."

	Jan.	Feb.	Mar.	Apr.	May	June	July	Aug.	Sept.	Oct.	Nov.	Dec.
pears	X	X	X	X	X	X	X	X	X	X	X	X
bananas	X	X	X	X	X	X	X	X	X	X	X	X
lemons	X	X	X	X	X	X	X	X	X	X	X	X
apples	X	X	X	X	X				X	X	X	X
grapefruit	X	X	X	X	X				X	X	X	X
oranges	X	X	X	X	X	X			X	X	X	X
peaches						X	X	X				
watermelon						X	X	X				
cherries						X	X	X				
berries						X	X	X				
grapes							X	X	X	X		

1. Are cherries cheap or expensive in January? _____

   _____

2. When can you buy bananas? _____

3. When is grapefruit in season? _____

4. When are peaches better, in the summer or in the fall?_____

   _____

5. Which fruits are summer fruits? _____

6. Which fruits are better in the fall? _____

7. Which fruits can you eat all year? _____

   _____

Exercise 4   Complete the sentences.

1. Fruit grows on _____ .

2. Most fruit has _____ .

3. Buy fruit that is _____ .

4. Do not buy _____ .

5. Fruit that is not in season is _____ .

6. Fresh fruits and vegetables _____ quickly.

7. When you touch the fruit don't _____ it.

8. The best time to buy apples is _____ .

9. The best time to buy watermelon is _____ .

10. The best time to buy grapes is _____ .

Exercise 5   Identify the pictures.

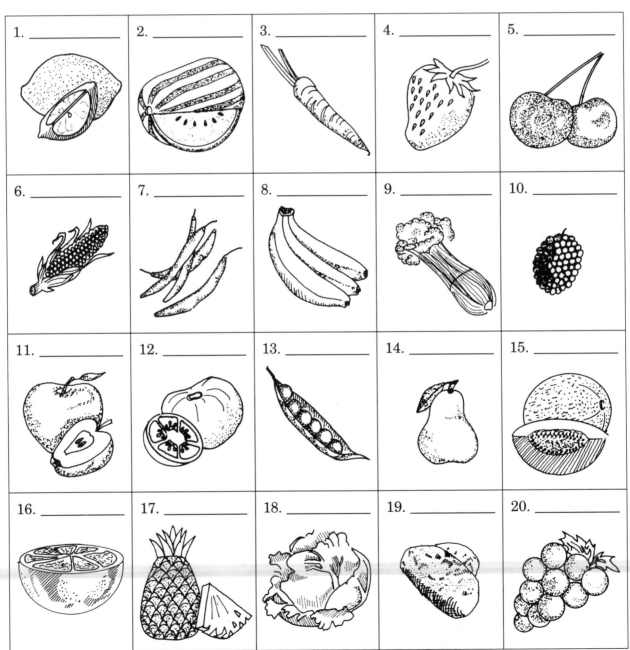

| 1. _____ | 2. _____ | 3. _____ | 4. _____ | 5. _____ |

| 6. _____ | 7. _____ | 8. _____ | 9. _____ | 10. _____ |

| 11. _____ | 12. _____ | 13. _____ | 14. _____ | 15. _____ |

| 16. _____ | 17. _____ | 18. _____ | 19. _____ | 20. _____ |

Everyday English, Book Three

Lesson **30** Shopping for Food

Exercise 1   Study these expressions.

1. a loaf of bread   5. a can of soup

2. a carton of milk   6. a tub / stick of butter

3. a box of eggs   7. a bag of sugar

4. a jar of jam

Exercise 2   Read the following dialogue.

Storekeeper: Good morning, Vivian.

Vivian: Good morning. I need a carton of milk, a box of eggs, a jar of strawberry jam, a can of pea soup, a pound of cheese, and a bag of sugar. Oh yes, I almost forgot: a loaf of bread.

Storekeeper: Here are the milk, eggs, jam, soup, cheese, and sugar. Do you want a large loaf of bread, or a small one?

Vivian: A large loaf please. How much are the eggs today?

Storekeeper: The eggs are 73¢ a dozen. Do you need cereal today?

Vivian: No, thank you. How much is my bill?

Storekeeper: That will be $7.51, please.

Vivian: Here's ten dollars.

Storekeeper: And here's your change.

Vivian: Thank you. So long.

Exercise 3   Complete the sentences.

1. Good _____ , Vivian.

2. _____ I have a carton of _____ , a

    _____ of eggs, a _____ of jam, a

    _____ of soup, a _____ of butter, and a

    _____ of bread.

3. Do you want a _____ loaf or a _____

    loaf?

4. A large _____ , please.

5. Eggs are _____ a dozen.

6. How much is my _____ ?

7. Vivian gives the storekeeper _____ .

8. The storekeeper gives her _____ change.

Exercise 4   Answer the questions with complete sentences.

1. What does the storekeeper say when the customer enters?

    _____

2. What does the customer need? _____

    _____

3. Does the customer want a large loaf of bread or a small loaf?

    _____

4. How much are eggs today? _____

5. Does the customer need cereal? _____

6. How much is the bill? _____

7. How much does the customer give the storekeeper?_____

Exercise 5   Write out the amount in words.

1. $ .45   _____

2.   25¢   _____

3. $1.00   _____

4. $4.65   _____

5. $3.99   _____

6. $ .19   _____

Exercise 6   Solve these problems.

1. If I buy a bottle of juice for $1.99, a box of cereal for 89¢, and a pie for

    $1.75, what is my bill? _____

2. If my bill is $4.98, and I give the storekeeper a ten-dollar bill, how

    much change do I get? _____

3. If oranges are four for a dollar, how much are two?

_____

Exercise 7   Make a list of things you need to buy at the grocery store.

1. _____   6. _____

2. _____   7. _____

3. _____   8. _____

4. _____   9. _____

5. _____   10. _____

Lesson 31 In a Restaurant

Exercise 1   Study the following sentences.

To *order* is to ask for.
A *menu* is a list of food you can order.
You can eat a small *appetizer* at the beginning of a meal.
The *entree* is the main dish.
Dessert is at the end of a meal.
A *waiter* is a man who takes your order.
A *waitress* is a woman who takes your order.

Exercise 2   Read the following dialogue with your teacher.

Danny is in a restaurant. He is ordering lunch.

Waiter: Are you ready to order, sir?

Danny: Please show me the menu.

Waiter: Here you are.

Danny: Thank you. *(After looking at the menu)* What kind of soup do you have today?

Waiter: Today we have pea soup and vegetable soup.

Danny: I'll have the pea soup, please. What's the special today?

Waiter: As an entree we have pot roast with carrots and potatoes.

Danny: Hmm . . . Please bring me a cheese omelet and a salad.

Waiter: What would you like to drink?

Danny: Just a glass of water, please.

Waiter: Do you want to order your dessert now or later?

Danny: I'll order now. I'll have some apple pie and a cup of coffee.

Waiter: Will that be all, sir?

Danny: Yes. Thank you very much.

Exercise 3   Complete the sentences.

1. Danny is in a _____ .

2. He needs a _____ to order his meal.

3. The _____ takes his order.

4. Danny wants _____ soup.

5. The special is _____ .

6. Danny orders a _____ and a _____ .

7. For dessert he orders _____ .

Exercise 4   Imagine that you and your friend are in a restaurant. Invent a dialogue between you and the waiter or waitress.

_____

_____

_____

_____

_____

_____

_____

_____

_____

_____

_____

_____

Exercise 5   True or False?

1. People often put milk and sugar in their coffee.   _____

2. Bacon is a fruit.   _____

3. Dinner is the meal you eat in the morning.   _____

4. Black coffee is coffee with milk or cream.   _____

5. If you overeat, you will lose weight.   _____

6. Ice cream is good on top of meat.   _____

7. The meal in the middle of the day is lunch.   _____

8. Ham, bacon, and sausage are all good with eggs.   _____

9. Some people like tea in the morning.   _____

Lesson **32** Food Day

Exercise 1   Read the following paragraph.

What are good foods to eat? Good foods are fish, meat, vegetables, and fruit, for example. *Junk* foods are chips, candy, *starches*, and *fats*. What should we look for when we buy food? We should make sure that the meat we buy doesn't have a lot of fat and bone. We should make sure that there are no dark spots on the fruits and vegetables. Make sure the date on the package of all foods is recent. *Comparison shop.* Look in more than one store. Try to stay away from artificial foods. Buy natural products. Remember, to be healthy we must think about the foods we eat.

Exercise 2   Answer the questions with complete sentences.

1. What are some good foods? _____

_____

2. What are some bad foods? _____

_____

3. What should you look for when you buy meat? _____

_____

4. What should you look for when you buy fruits and vegetables?

   _____

5. What should you look for when you buy all foods? _____

   _____

6. What do we mean by *comparison shop?* _____

   _____

Exercise 3   Bring a simple recipe that is popular in your native country.

1. Is the food for breakfast, lunch, or dinner? _____

2. What basic food group does it belong to? _____

3. Is it an appetizer, an entree, or a dessert? _____

4. Is it a snack? _____

5. What beverage do you like to drink with it? _____

Lesson **33** Nutrition

Exercise 1   Read the following paragraphs and chart.

Food gives us energy. It gives us nutrients to grow and to repair our bodies. It gives us carbohydrates, fats, proteins, vitamins, minerals, and water. These nutrients are the body's building blocks. The nutrients must be digested to become a few simple chemicals. This is what gives us energy. This is also what keeps our body temperature at 98.6 degrees Fahrenheit.

In this chart, you will see some examples of foods that provide carbohydrates, fats, proteins, vitamins, and minerals.

Fuel — Carbohydrates / Fats

bread	butter
cake	bacon
rice	milk
pasta	cream
potatoes	chocolate

Building Block — Protein

poultry	fish
milk	meat
vegetables	eggs
nuts	

Regulation of Body Processes — Vitamins and Minerals

berries	milk
fish	citrus fruit (oranges, grapefruit)
eggs	green vegetables

Vitamin	*helps*	*found in*
Vitamin A	vision	carrots
Vitamin B	us to grow, gives us an appetite	wheat germ
Vitamin C	strengthen gums, fight colds	citrus fruit
Vitamin D	build bones and teeth	milk
Vitamin K	clot blood	spinach

Mineral	*helps*	*found in*
Iron	build red blood cells	liver
Calcium	teeth, bones	
Phosphorus	teeth, bones	milk

Exercise 2 Match the words with their definitions.

A	B
____ 1. energy	a. fix
____ 2. repair	b. broken down by the body
____ 3. regulate	c. control
____ 4. nutrients	d. strength
____ 5. digested	e. food

Exercise 3   Circle the words that best complete the sentences.

1. Vitamin A helps our _____ .

   a. tests   b. eyesight   c. feet

2. Potatoes are rich in _____ .

   a. calcium   b. protein   c. carbohydrates

3. A(n) _____ is a citrus fruit.

   a. apple   b. orange   c. pear

4. Liver contains a lot of _____ .

   a. iron   b. fat   c. carbohydrates

5. Lemons contain a lot of _____ .

   a. Vitamin A   b. Vitamin B   c. Vitamin C

6. One of the best all-around foods is _____ .

   a. cream   b. milk   c. candy

7. _____ are fuel for our bodies.

   a. carbohydrates b. proteins   c. vitamins

8. A lot of Vitamin D is found in _____ .

   a. fruit   b. milk   c. liver

9. Carrots have a lot of Vitamin _____ .

   a. A   b. B   c. C

10. To build our bones and teeth we need _____ .

   a. Vitamin D   b. spinach   c. fish

Lesson 34 Review of Food

Exercise 1   Complete the sentences.

1. _____ is a meat product.

2. _____ is a fish product.

3. _____ is a poultry product.

4. _____ is a fruit product.

Everyday English, Book Three

5. _____ is a citrus product.

6. _____ is a vegetable product.

7. _____ is a dairy product.

8. We usually eat _____ meals a day:

_____ in the morning, _____ at noon,

and _____ in the evening.

Exercise 2   Answer with complete sentences.

1. Give an example of an appetizer. _____

_____

2. Give an example of an entree. _____

_____

3. Give an example of a beverage. _____

_____

4. Give an example of a dessert. _____

_____

5. What time do you eat breakfast? lunch? dinner? a snack?_____

_____

_____

6. In the United States, which is usually the biggest meal of the day?

_____

_____

7. Why is it important to have a good breakfast?_____

_____

8. What do you eat for breakfast? for lunch? for dinner? _____

_____

_____

_____

Exercise 3   Find and circle the hidden words from the list. They may read across, down, diagonally, forward, or backward. Then find the four letters you do not use. Put them in order to spell the mystery word.

grapefruit	steak	fish	pea	stew
sausage	tuna	apple	berry (2)	bun
milk	cream	meat	salt	soy
cookies	plum	gum	tart	root
bread	cereal	pie	tea	fin
				are

G	C	O	O	K	I	E	S	S	S
C	R	S	T	E	W	M	B	T	A
E	E	A	P	P	L	E	R	E	U
R	A	L	P	E	A	A	E	A	S
E	M	T	I	E	F	T	A	K	A
A	T	E	E	B	F	O	D	O	G
L	O	A	E	U	H	R	T	K	E
S	O	R	R	N	S	M	U	L	P
O	R	D	A	T	I	U	N	I	F
Y	R	R	E	B	F	G	A	M	T

Mystery Word: _____

Exercise 4   Find brand names for:

1. oranges _____   6. tuna _____

2. cookies _____   7. ice cream _____

3. frozen peas _____   8. yogurt _____

4. juice _____   9. milk _____

5. salad dressing _____   10. rice _____

Exercise 5   Write a commercial for a favorite food. Tell why it is good and why the
public should buy it.

_____

_____

_____

_____

_____

_____

_____

_____

_____

_____

Exercise 6   Write to a friend in your native country and tell him or her what you eat
for breakfast, lunch, and dinner. Tell how your American meals are
different from the meals you ate in your native country.

_____

_____

_____

_____

_____

_____

_____

_____

_____

_____

_____

_____

_____

Unit
6 Animals

Lesson 35 Names of Animals

Exercise 1   Study the following vocabulary.

dog	camel	pig	bird
monkey	chicken	cow	lion
whale	kangaroo	snake	deer
dinosaur	octopus	horse	duck

bear	frog	cat	turtle
giraffe	tiger	elephant	zebra
bee	rat	shark	fly
fox	spider	rabbit	sheep
butterfly	goat	ant	owl

Exercise 2   Complete these names of animals. Use the vocabulary from exercise 1 to help you.

1. __ __ R T __ __

2. H __ __ S __

3. __ __ O G

4. K __ __ G A __ __ O

5. __ __ N K __ __

6. __ I G __ R

7. __ __ __ A F F __

8. C __ __

9. __ __ __ C K E __

10. __ A B B __ __

11. __ A __ E __

12. __ E E R

13. __ __ T O __ __ S

14. __ O W

15. D __ __ K

16. __ __ __ P H A __ __

17. __ N __

18. __ __ __ K E

19. B __ __ D

20. __ I O __

Exercise 3   Unscramble the animal names and write them in the boxes. Then unscramble the circled letters to find the mystery words.

a c t

f a i g r f e

a r t

d r i b

Mystery Word: _____

o y k m n e

l a m e c

s h i f

Mystery Word: _____

Lesson 36 Classes of Animals

Exercise 1 Read the following paragraphs.

Tomorrow we will go to the zoo. At the zoo we will see many *classes* of animals. Mammals are animals that are warm-blooded. Their body temperatures are always the same. They develop inside their mothers' bodies. They drink their mothers' milk. Human beings are mammals. Dogs, elephants, monkeys, and lions are other mammals.

We will see *birds*. Birds are also warm-blooded, but they lay eggs. They live on land, in trees, or near water. Eagles, parrots, and peacocks are birds.

We will also see *reptiles*. Reptiles are cold-blooded. The temperature of their blood changes with the climate. Baby reptiles hatch from eggs. They have scaly skin. Snakes and turtles are reptiles.

We will see *amphibians*, too. They can live in water and on land. Frogs are amphibians.

Then we will see *fish*. fish live in the water. Sharks and tuna are different types of fish. Don't be fooled: whales are mammals!

We will also see *insects* such as spiders, ants, and bees. We'll have a good time!

Exercise 2 Can you name the six classes of animals? Refer to exercise 1.

1. _____   3. _____   5. _____

2. _____   4. _____   6. _____

List three animals for each class. Refer to exercise 1.

1. _____   3. _____   5. _____

   _____   _____   _____

   _____   _____   _____

2. _____   4. _____   6. _____

   _____   _____   _____

   _____   _____   _____

Exercise 3 Study the vocabulary in the following sentences.

1. *Warm-blooded* means that body temperature doesn't change. Human beings are warm-blooded. Their body temperature is normally 98.6 degrees.

2. *Cold-blooded* means that body temperature changes with the climate. Snakes are cold-blooded.

3. *Scaly* skin is not smooth.

4. Snakes, dogs, and frogs belong to different *classes* or groups of animals.

Give two examples of warm-blooded animals. _____

_____

Give two examples of cold-blooded animals. _____

_____

Exercise 4 Match the antonyms.

A	B
____ 1. different	a. inside
____ 2. outside	b. land
____ 3. scaly	c. die
____ 4. always	d. few
____ 5. water	e. smooth
____ 6. don't	f. far
____ 7. live	g. same
____ 8. near	h. bad
____ 9. good	i. do
____ 10. many	j. never

Exercise 5   Complete the story.

The six classes of animals are _____ , _____ ,

_____ , _____ , _____ , _____ ,

and _____ . Mammals are _____ - _____

animals. Their temperature never _____ . _____ ,

_____ , and _____ are mammals. Reptiles are

_____ - _____ animals. They have

_____ skin. _____ and _____ are

reptiles. Amphibians live on _____ and in the

_____ . _____ are amphibians. Fish live in the

_____ . _____ and _____ are fish.

_____ and _____ are insects. Birds

_____ eggs. They live in _____ , on

_____ , or near _____ . _____ and

_____ are birds. Whales are _____.. Human beings

are also _____ .

Lesson 37 More About Animals

Exercise 1   Study the vocabulary in the following sentences.

    1. Some animals are *wild*. They live in a natural setting like the forest or the jungle. Lions and tigers are wild animals.

    2. Some animals are *tame*. That means they are gentle enough to live around people. Cats and dogs are tame animals.

    3. Tame animals make good *pets*. Wild animals do not. Pets are animals that people keep for pleasure.

Exercise 2   Answer the questions with complete sentences.

1. Where do rabbits live? _____

_____

2. Are bears wild animals?_____

_____

3. Where do chickens and pigs live?_____

_____

4. Name three wild animals _____

_____

5. Name three animals that are usually tame. _____

_____

6. Can a tiger be a pet? _____

_____

7. Where do camels live? _____

_____

Exercise 3   Complete the sentences.

1. _____ fly.   4. _____ chase rats.

2. _____ live in the water.   5. _____ chase cats.

6. _____ eat cheese.

Exercise 4   Give examples of animals that:

1. are small. _____

_____

2. are large. _____

_____

3. live in water. _____

_____

4. walk on two legs. _____

_____

5. walk on four legs. _____

_____

6. fly. _____

7. you can have in your house. _____

Lesson **38** The Pet Shop

Exercise 1 Use the following questions to help you invent a dialogue about a visit to the pet shop.

1. What do you say when you enter?
2. What does the pet shop clerk answer?
3. What would you like?
4. How much does it cost?
5. Is it too expensive?
6. How you use it / take care of it?
7. Will you buy it?
8. How much change do you get?
9. What do you and the clerk say when you leave?

_____

_____

_____

_____

_____

_____

_____

_____

_____

_____

Exercise 2   Now make up five questions about your dialogue.

1. _____

2. _____

3. _____

4. _____

5. _____

Exercise 3   Find the plurals of these animal names. Use your dictionary to help you.

1. goose   _____   6. fly   _____

2. sheep   _____   7. monkey   _____

3. fish   _____   8. bear   _____

4. deer   _____   9. butterfly   _____

5. mouse   _____   10. horse   _____

Exercise 4   Match column A and column B.

A	B
____ 1. dinosaurs	a. look like horses with stripes
____ 2. sharks	b. live in the water and have sharp teeth
____ 3. monkeys	c. sleep all winter
____ 4. zebras	d. have big ears and eat peanuts
____ 5. butterflies	e. are big cats with stripes
____ 6. elephants	f. lived many, many years ago
____ 7. camels	g. have humps on their backs
____ 8. bears	h. fly
____ 9. tigers	i. climb trees and eat bananas

Everyday English, Book Three

Lesson **39** Male, Female, and Baby Animals

Exercise 1   Write the names of the female animals.

1. lion   _____   5. bull   _____

2. tiger   _____   6. rooster   _____

3. stallion   _____   7. stag   _____

4. ram   _____   8. gander   _____

Exercise 2   Complete the sentences.

1. A male chicken is a rooster. A female chicken is a _____ .

2. A male sheep is a ram. A female sheep is a _____ .

3. A male deer is a _____ . A female deer is a _____ .

4. Male cattle are _____ . Female cattle are _____ .

5. A male horse is a _____ . A female horse is a _____ .

Exercise 3   Match the animal to its "baby" name.

A	**B**
____ 1. cat	a. kid
____ 2. dog	b. kitten
____ 3. chicken	c. gosling
____ 4. goat	d. lamb
____ 5. sheep	e. puppy
____ 6. goose	f. chick
____ 7. pig	g. fawn
____ 8. deer	h. cub
____ 9. tiger	i. piglet
____ 10. duck	j. duckling

Exercise 4   Choose the words that best complete the sentences.

1. A cow says _____ .   a. oink   b. quack   c. moo   d. cluck
2. A lion says _____ .   a. roar   b. moo   c. arf   d. oink
3. A pig says _____ .   a. oink   b. neigh   c. roar   d. chirp
4. A duck says _____ .   a. meow   b. roar   c. moo   d. quack
5. A hen says _____ .   a. baa   b. oink   c. cluck   d. arf
6. A horse says _____ .   a. neigh   b. meow   c. cluck   d. quack
7. A dog says _____ .   a. meow   b. bow-wow   c. oink   d. roar
8. A cat says _____ .   a. neigh   b. roar   c. meow   d. oink
9. A bird says _____ .   a. chirp   b. meow   c. neigh   d. roar
10. A sheep says _____ .   a. baa   b. neigh   c. oink   d. quack

Lesson **40** Review of Animals

Exercise 1   Answer with complete sentences.

1. Name the six classes of animals. _____

_____

2. Name two animals in each class. _____

_____

3. What class of animal do human beings belong to?_____

_____

4. What class does the whale belong to? _____

_____

5. What does *cold-blooded* mean?_____

_____

6. What does *warm-blooded* mean? _____

_____

7. What is a human being's normal temperature? _____

_____

8. What are tame animals? _____

_____

Everyday English, Book Three

9. What are wild animals? _____

_____

10. What is a pet? _____

_____

Exercise 2   Complete the sentences.

1. A _____ is a wild animal.

2. A _____ is a tame animal.

3. A _____ makes a good pet.

4. A _____ is a cold-blooded animal.

5. A _____ is a warm-blooded animal.

6. The _____ is extinct (no longer living).

7. A _____ flies.

8. A _____ lives in the water.

9. A _____ lives in the water and on land.

10. A _____ climbs trees.

11. A _____ has a hump on its back.

12. A _____ has a long neck.

13. An _____ has big ears.

14. A _____ has black and white stripes.

Exercise 3   Match the male and female animals.

A	B
____ 1. rooster	a. lioness
____ 2. gander	b. ewe
____ 3. lion	c. tigress
____ 4. stag	d. doe
____ 5. tiger	e. mare
____ 6. bull	f. goose
____ 7. ram	g. elephant (cow)
____ 8. stallion	h. cow
____ 9. elephant (bull)	i. hen

Exercise 4   Complete the chart.

Animal	Baby	Sound
1. cat	_____	_____
2. cow	_____	_____
3. dog	_____	_____
4. sheep	_____	_____
5. duck	_____	_____
6. horse	_____	_____
7. lion	_____	_____
8. tiger	_____	_____
9. pig	_____	_____
10. chicken	_____	_____

Exercise 5   Find and circle the hidden words from the list. They may read across, down, diagonally, forward, or backward.

dinosaur
elephant
bee
deer
ant
gander
dog
lion
rabbit
fox
chicken
cat
mare
baa
owl
roach
fish
colt
doe
bird
chirp
bear
bull
hen
cow
whale

L	L	U	B	R	E	T	S	O	O	R	E	E
A	W	D	W	I	O	A	G	R	C	O	L	T
M	F	O	X	O	R	A	E	I	A	E	A	S
M	C	E	S	P	E	D	C	H	P	N	H	E
A	C	A	T	H	N	M	A	H	S	A	W	R
M	O	O	A	A	B	E	A	E	I	I	E	A
T	E	L	G	I	P	N	K	R	R	T	F	M
I	N	D	A	P	T	M	A	C	S	D	O	G
G	B	E	E	I	I	B	N	O	I	L	W	E
E	S	E	E	G	B	R	O	N	E	H	L	W
R	H	R	A	I	F	R	P	R	I	H	C	E
S	A	N	T	R	D	I	N	O	S	A	U	R

ewe   meow   geese   stag
moo   sheep   tigers   mammal
rooster (2)   pig   piglet   ram

Exercise 6   Complete this crossword puzzle.

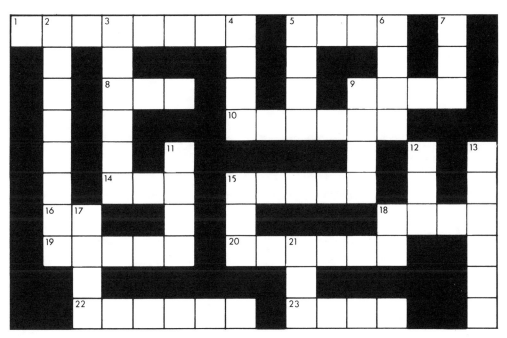

Across

1 Turtles and snakes are _____ .

5 A baby sheep is a _____ .

8 A male sheep is a _____ .

9 A _____ goat is a kid.

10 A male goose is a _____ .

14 A female sheep is a _____ .

15 Baby horses are _____ .

16 Are you a pig? _____ , I'm not.

18 _____ are insects.

19 A baby _____ is a cub.

20 _____ are not fish. They

    are mammals.

22 A baby cat is a _____ .

23 A tuna is a _____ .

Down

2 An _____ is an immense animal.

3 A _____ is a reptile.

4 A male deer is a _____ .

5 A _____ says "roar."

6 A baby _____ is a cub.

7 A _____ is an insect.

9 _____ are insects that make honey.

11 Does and stags are _____ .

12 A _____ says "cluck."

13 A spider is an _____ .

15 A _____ gives us milk.

17 A pig says " _____ ."

18 A dinosaur is as big _____ a house.

21 A dog says "bow-wow" or " _____ ."